D1277556

THE
WHITE POWER
MOVEMENT

THE WHITE POWER

MOVEMENT

AMERICA'S RACIST HATE GROUPS

BY ELAINE LANDAU

The Millbrook Press
Brookfield, Connecticut

Photos courtesy of: AP/Wide World Photos: pp. 11, 16, 35, 54; Anti-Defamation League: p. 19; Library of Congress: p. 25 (both); R. B. Hayes Presidential Center, Fremont, Ohio: p. 26; UPI/Bettmann: pp. 30, 38, 48, 57, 76; © Leonard Freed/Magnum Photos: pp. 42, 45; © Mark Richards: p. 53; Gamma Liaison: p. 68 (Harris); Reuters/Bettmann: p. 71; © Michael Kienitz, Picture Group: p. 79; Karen Pike Riesner: p. 82.

Library of Congress Cataloging-in-Publication Data

Landau, Elaine.
The White power movement : America's racist hate groups / by Elaine Landau.
p. cm.
Includes bibliographical reference (p.   ) and index.
Summary: Explores the origins and development of racist hate groups in the United States, such as the Ku Klux Klan and the skinheads.
ISBN 1-56294-327-8 (lib. bdg.)
1. White supremacy movements—United States—History—Juvenile literature. 2. United States—Race relations—Juvenile literature.
[1. White supremacy movements. 2. Racism. 3. Race relations. 4. Prejudices.] I. Title.
E184.A1L255 1993
305.8'00973—dc20   92-40920 CIP AC

Published by The Millbrook Press
2 Old New Milford Road
Brookfield, Connecticut 06804

CONTENTS

THE
WHITE POWER
MOVEMENT

ONE
A HATE WAVE

The trouble began early in the morning on a sunny Saturday, May 26, 1979. Just after dawn, members of the Ku Klux Klan gathered in small groups throughout Alabama. From their various towns and villages, they set out for Decatur, an industrial city in the northern central part of the state. Their mission was to assist in what their leader, a man known as the Grand Dragon, referred to as "stopping the niggers." [1]

The Klansmen were armed. While their most deadly weapons that day included rifles, pistols, and machetes, members had also outfitted themselves with an assortment of other tools for violence: tire irons, two-by-fours, tree limbs, ax handles, and baseball bats.

The Klan planned to disrupt a march by Decatur's African-American community to protest the 1978 arrest and conviction of Tommy Lee Hines, a twenty-six-year-old mentally retarded African American whom the protest-

[9

ers believed had been wrongfully accused of robbing and raping three white women.

This was not the community's first protest of Hines's conviction. On numerous other occasions, hundreds of demonstrators had marched down the same streets to focus national attention on what they viewed as an obvious case of injustice.

The marchers had planned the May 26 event in advance and were promised ample police protection by local authorities. But that had not deterred the Klan. The organization was enraged over the attention Hines had received and was determined to stop it once and for all.

As the morning wore on, small groups of Klansmen began arriving at the appointed meeting place, the northern bank of the Tennessee River just across from Decatur. After greeting one another, those especially anxious to launch their attack on the African Americans donned their traditional costumes—white hoods and robes—and readied their weapons. One Klan member passed out spare ax handles, while another busied himself carving a club out of a nearby tree limb. A few feet away, other Klansmen proudly displayed a makeshift gallows, a platform used for hanging, constructed in the back of a pickup truck. From the gallows a cloth dummy, supposedly Tommy Lee Hines, dangled.

The Klan members were not concerned about the police interrupting their assault on the marchers. In the past, local law-enforcement officials had presented little resistance to their activities, and the Klan had come to believe it could violate the law freely.

Tommy Lee Hines, center, is taken into court in Cullman, Alabama, to stand trial on charges of raping and robbing white women.

After reviewing its final orders, a Klan caravan consisting of nearly thirty cars and pickup trucks made its way across the bridge to Decatur. Meanwhile the African-American protesters were disappointedly assessing the number of people who had turned out for the march. Although close to five hundred demonstrators had swarmed into the courthouse area for the initial protests following Hines's conviction, that Saturday less than sixty came to the same spot.

Some believed the diminished number was at least partly due to the intimidation tactics that the Klan had directed against the African-American community throughout the year. When the Klan burned a cross in front of Decatur's City Hall, close to five thousand people attended, vowing to stop the public displays of sympathy for Hines. On another occasion an African-American preacher was kidnapped by Klan members at a pro-Hines demonstration and severely beaten. At other times, vehicles carrying groups of Klansmen cruised through African-American neighborhoods as a reminder of the Klan's continued presence.

Despite such threats Tommy Lee Hines's supporters began their mile-long march through Decatur that May 26. Anticipating the Klan confrontation, local newspaper and television reporters were on the scene to record the event. Only a handful of others dotted the streets, since it was Saturday and the march was held in a fairly quiet part of town.

Just before the marchers reached their halfway mark, a wave of Klansmen in their robes and hoods appeared. The marchers continued, even though the only barrier separating them from the Klan was a slender line of local police and county deputies. Tension mounted as the demonstrators' freedom songs were drowned out by such racial taunts as "Stop the niggers," "Kill the niggers," and "Nigger, you ain't going past here."[2]

Moments later dozens of armed Klansmen surged forward to physically block the marchers. But things did not go as the Klan had planned. This time the police tried to stop its members. It was later learned that Decatur leaders, who had on previous occasions declined to interrupt Klan activities, had decided to do so now to preserve their city's image. A scuffle between the lawmen and the Klan ensued, but the police were at a distinct disadvantage since they were not equipped with riot gear or tear gas and the Klansmen outnumbered them two to one.

Although the police were unable to completely clear the marchers' path, they managed to keep open a small corridor for the demonstrators. Thinking that they might be able to complete their march after all, the protesters continued to move slowly forward. But soon another wave of Klansmen flooded the street making it impossible for them to go on. Tommy Lee Hines's supporters had no choice but to stand back on the sidewalk and watch the police battle the Klan.

Suddenly, the scuffling turned seriously violent. Some Klansmen unexpectedly fired their guns into the crowd. The police stopped the shooting, but by the time it was over four people had been seriously wounded.

The protesters, who never finished their march that day, were determined not to be controlled by the Klan. Just two weeks following the incident, more than 1,500 civil rights activists from various parts of the country gathered in Decatur to help complete the demonstration.

The issue at stake had become larger than Tommy Lee Hines's case. It was now a question of whether all Americans had the right to freely assemble without being subjected to outside intimidation. Though nearly 250 robed Klansmen came to jeer and taunt the marchers, this time the protesters were protected by hundreds of police officers and National Guardsmen. It was a proud day for those who had fought long and hard against racially motivated violence.

HATE ON THE RISE Although the 1960s civil rights movement had not resulted in the complete dissolution of organizations like the Klan, many people—such as those who helped to complete the march for Tommy Lee Hines—had hoped that by the end of the 1970s these groups might be losing their effectiveness and appeal. Such expectations proved overly optimistic. Hate crimes—acts of violence motivated by racial prejudice, such as the Decatur incident—actually increased during the late 1970s and throughout the 1980s. Hate crimes, in fact, remained on the rise in the early 1990s. America has been experiencing a surge in white-power activism.

White power is a phrase that describes a belief held by the Ku Klux Klan and other individuals and groups. These people believe that white Americans whose families originated in Western European countries such as England and Germany deserve to possess power over people from other areas. Why? According to these people, such white Americans are "naturally" superior—hence the notion of white supremacy.

The Ku Klux Klan holds that whites are particularly superior to African Americans. They especially fear any mixing between whites and African Americans that would make whites "impure," less superior, and therefore less powerful. For this reason, they were contemptuous of Tommy Lee Hines, an African American who supposedly had sex with white women.

But the Decatur episode represents only one aspect of the Klan's broad scope of hatred. It holds in contempt people of a variety of races and religions, particularly Jews. It disdains many immigrant groups, which, it believes, also make America "less white." In short, its members despise anyone unlike themselves.

Acting from this platform of prejudicial ideas, the Klan has helped foster America's growing climate of hate. Here are just a few examples:

— In 1986 the Ku Klux Klan planned to hold a homecoming march in Pulaski, Tennessee, where the organization originated. However, the Pulaski town council initially denied the Klan a parade permit. Some thought the march might be canceled, until the Grand Wizard, the leader of the group, threatened to sue both the city council and any council member who voted against the event. After reviewing the situation, the town attorney determined that the city was required by law to issue the parade permit. On January 18, Martin Luther King, Jr., Day, Klan men, women, and young people, dressed in their robes and pointed hats, marched through Pulaski's streets

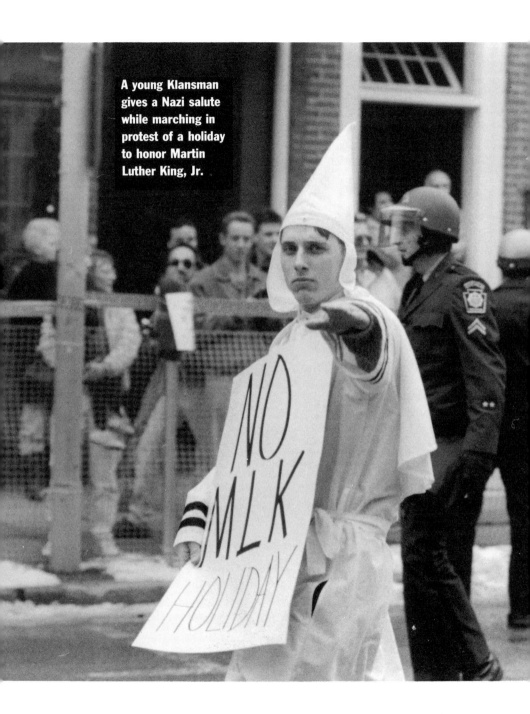

A young Klansman gives a Nazi salute while marching in protest of a holiday to honor Martin Luther King, Jr.

to protest the national holiday as well as to honor the man convicted of Dr. King's assassination, James Earl Ray. On more than one occasion the group had described Dr. King as a Communist and Ray as a true American.

- At a 1991 rally in Arkansas, Klan leaders passed out cloths bearing the Star of David, a Jewish religious symbol, which they referred to as "Jewish flags." They encouraged participants to use the flags "for blowing noses, wiping feet or burning."[3] Klan speakers also bitterly complained about the "curse of immigration," which they perceived as overwhelming the country with non-European people.

While for many years the Klan was generally considered the largest and most active hate organization in America, more recently new, similarly minded groups have flourished. During the early 1990s it was estimated that between 400 and 450 white-supremacist organizations existed in the United States.[4] Here is just a sampling of their activities and the range of their targets.

- In 1988 in Chicago, Illinois, white-supremacist youths, known as racist skinheads, knocked a twenty-year-old Jewish woman to the ground and severely beat and kicked her. Before leaving the injured woman where she lay, they painted a swastika, a symbol of German Nazism, on a nearby wall with her blood.

- In 1987 in San José, California, another racist skinhead group stopped a fifty-year-old African-American schoolteacher as she approached a footbridge in a public park. After informing her that "niggers" were to pay a toll, they threatened to hang her from a nearby tree if she did not comply with their demands for money. One of the skinheads later arrested for the incident described their motivation as follows, "We are racial and she was Black. . . . We're into white supremacy."[5]

— In 1988 in Atlanta, Georgia, white supremacist skinheads chanted anti-gay epithets as they beat two women they suspected of being lesbians. Before leaving they also smashed the women's car windows with a brick.

— Four members of the white supremacist Idaho-based organization, Bruder Schweigen Strike Force Two (Bruder Schweigen is German for Silent Brotherhood), pleaded guilty to a September 1988 bombing of the residence of a Roman Catholic priest who had frequently criticized the hate group. Several weeks later the same organization set off two other homemade bombs. One exploded outside a federal office building that served as Federal Bureau of Investigation (FBI) headquarters.

— A California organization founded in 1980, the Institute for Historical Review (I.H.R.), asserted that the German Nazi-generated Holocaust never took place. The group is one of a network of groups controlled by Willis Carto, who runs Liberty Lobby, a Washington, D.C., anti-Semitic organization. I.H.R. sponsors conventions and prints books and articles that argue that classic Holocaust books such as Anne Frank's *Diary*

The Journal of Historical Review

Carlo Mattogno
The Myth of the Extermination of the Jews

Mark Weber
An Open Letter to the Rev. Mark Herbener

Paul Grubach
A Critique of the Charge of Anti-Semitism

Martin Merson
On the Treadmill to Truth

—Reviews—

Waldheim • *Stalin's War* • *An American in Exile*
Heckling Hitler • *Keeper of Concentration Camps*
Marxism in the United States

—Historical News and Comment—

West Germany's Holocaust Payoff to Israel and World Jewry
Pearl Harbor Survivors Association Honors Kimmel and Short

VOLUME EIGHT, NUMBER TWO   SUMMER 1988

As this page from an I.H.R. publication indicates, the group denies the occurrence of the Holocaust.

of a Young Girl are untrue. The group also charges that photographs of Nazi concentration camps and survivor testimonials have been falsified.

— In 1987 at the University of Chicago, white supremacists painted swastikas on the doors of several student residence halls. The incident was just one in a series of hate crimes perpetrated by an organization called the Great White Brotherhood of the Iron Fist. Other intimidation tactics employed by the group included making obscene phone calls and death threats to targeted gay students and liberal faculty members.

TECHNO-HATE White-power groups in the United States have not only grown more prevalent, they have also grown more sophisticated. Many have relied on state-of-the-art technology to reach a broader audience. As early as 1983 some groups were employing computers to establish white-supremacist communication networks. These far-reaching systems could be put into operation with a home computer, software, a device for transmitting computer information via phone called a modem, and a standard telephone line. They could be accessed twenty-four hours a day by anyone with a computer, a modem, communications software, and the network's phone number.

White-power computer networks have operated in Illinois, Wisconsin, California, Texas, Idaho, and West Virginia. One example of the typical white-supremacist electronic message is the following notice of the American National Socialist Party in Milwaukee: "This is the ultimate weapon that a beleaguered people (Whites) can resort to against (their) own government . . . when the situation has become desperate and intolerable. That weapon is terrorism and violence, taking the law into their own hands."[6]

Some groups specifically aim their messages at youths, believing that many young people spend a good deal of time unsupervised at their home computers. They also feel that a young, impressionable audience might be more readily moved to their way of thinking.

Hate groups have seized upon other technological advances as well. While many cities have telephone services with which callers can get the time, weather, or sports scores, white-supremacist organizations have adapted this concept to advance their causes. One such phone line criticizes Dr. Martin Luther King, Jr., Day; another advocates violence to preserve racial purity.

Bigotry and racism are still alive and well in America. A major study commissioned by the National Council of Churches and conducted by the Atlanta-based Center for Democratic Renewal indicated that "harassment, vandalism, arson, assault, and murder motivated by racism, anti-Semitism, and other forms of bigotry—such as homophobia (dislike of homosexuals)—plague every section of our country."[7] It further categorizes such violence as a "largely unrecognized cancer eating away at our communities and social institutions."[8] A hate wave has been rising steadily in the United States.

TWO
THE WAVE'S ORIGINS AND THE KU KLUX KLAN

One of the forces behind the United States's hate wave and the hate crimes that go along with it is racism. Racism is the belief that one group of people is naturally superior to another because of its abilities or physical characteristics.

Racism appears to have been present even at the very founding of modern civilization. During the 1500s Western European explorers set out to conquer large portions of Asia, Africa, and the Americas. These explorers justified seizing lands from the peoples who already lived on them by proclaiming that these natives—many of whom were dark-skinned or physically different—were inferior. To excuse their own injustice and often brutality, conquering whites argued that exposing natives to European civilization and Christianity would improve them—thus helping to develop the notion of white supremacy.

AN AMERICAN TRADITION? Racism in the United States extends back to the nation's beginnings as well. Africans were brought as slaves to the British colonies in North America in the 1600s. Once again, the notion that these Africans were somehow subhuman was used to justify and perpetuate their enslavement. While lawmakers later attempted to remedy social and economic inequalities between African Americans and the white majority, racist attitudes toward people of color often persisted.

The philosophy of white superiority and contempt for people who are different have been promoted in the United States at the peril of not only African Americans. Although the United States has sometimes been referred to as a melting pot, since its society is a mixture of people from other parts of the world, nearly all of the immigrants who make up the society have faced a good deal of prejudice and racism. When masses of Irish immigrants arrived in the 1800s, many of the newcomers had to deal with taunts, harassment, and violence. They were automatically disliked and mistrusted because they were Catholics. Many perceived the Irish immigrants' willingness to work for a low wage in order to survive as an economic threat. More than half a century later, the many Chinese immigrants who came to the West Coast encountered similar, perhaps even more virulent, reactions.

Japanese, Jews, Italians, and Hispanics—all at one time newcomers to the United States—have met with hostility. The fear that newcomers would ruin employment prospects for those already established in the country, coupled with a general suspiciousness of people whose skin colors, languages, and cultures differed, led to incidents of violence.

Above: An early example of white power philosophy at work: African captives are auctioned off as slaves in the United States. Right: This 1882 cartoon reflects the racist stereotypes many Americans held of Irish immigrants. It depicts them as brutes who work at menial tasks.

This photo of two early Klan members was taken in 1868 at the height of the first wave of Klan activity in the United States.

THE BIRTH OF THE KKK

The Ku Klux Klan was the first major, violence-prone group in the United States to be organized according to racism in general and a belief in white supremacy in particular. It began in Tennessee shortly after the Civil War. A small group of discouraged and defeated Confederate soldiers banded together under the leadership of a former Confederate general, Nathan Bedford Forrest. They sought to maintain the practices of the old South—most notably the enslavement of African Americans—in the face of changes brought about by intruding Northerners and freed slaves. While at first these often unemployed ex-soldiers engaged largely in prankish stunts, before long the organization expanded and involved itself in increasingly violent and sinister activities.

Since most Klan members wore robes and hoods during Klan activities to conceal their identities, the organization became known as the Invisible Empire. By the late 1860s, these nameless men were actively engaged in their own campaign of brutality and terror throughout the South and bordering states. Lawless groups of Klansmen threatened, beat, mutilated, and lynched (hanged) African Americans as well as whites who dared to oppose them.

United by their shared racist ideals and the desire to preserve the old South, Klansmen consistently supported one another in their illegal exploits. Before long, however, their brutal deeds became increasingly random.

To stem the increasing frequency of the group's crimes in 1871, Congress passed legislation authorizing the president to use federal troops against the Klan. Klansmen blamed non-Klansmen for the murders and other atrocities attributed to them.

Meanwhile, membership sharply declined. By the mid-1870s only remnants of the first Ku Klux Klan remained.

1915–1940: A PERIOD OF GROWTH Several decades later, in 1915, the racist organization blossomed for a second time as political and economic conditions became ideal for its return. Product prices in many of the country's rural farm districts were down, leaving many farm owners and workers in economic difficulty and making them extremely susceptible to the Klan's racist message of how "Jewish bankers" and various outside foreign interests had played havoc with America's economy.

The Klan also gained a firm foothold in parts of the North and West where industrial and social changes, as well as the increased migration of African Americans from the South, had begun to make some less affluent whites increasingly insecure about their jobs. Billing the Klan as an organization exclusively geared for "real American men," the group drew new recruits seeking to recapture the power and control they believed they had lost in their everyday lives due to African Americans and new immigrants.

Besides its disdain for and frequent persecution of African Americans, Jews, Catholics, and foreigners, the Klan also punished white Protestant women it deemed immoral. A single woman thought to be a seductress might be unmercifully beaten, while adulterous wives often met a similar fate.

The Klan also did not look kindly on divorce. In 1927, a group of local Alabama Klansmen beat a divorced woman who had just remarried a divorced man. When the intense flogging was over, the men took up a collection for the woman and left her with a salve for her wounds. Before leaving, the Baptist minister who had led the group reminded her that the punishment had been administered "in a spirit of kindness and correction to set your feet aright." [1]

Protestant men and women who neglected their families felt the Klan's wrath as well. Klansmen in Indianapolis severely whipped one woman who had been arrested for child neglect, while Oklahoma Klansmen came after a father for failing to adequately provide for his family. As one townsperson described the incident: "They took the guy out and laid the leather to him, because he wasn't taking care of his family. Well, he got a job right quick and started working." [2]

The Klan's most hideously violent acts were reserved for nonwhite, foreign-born, and non-Protestant men who became involved with white Protestant women. Such men were the victims of kidnappings, beatings, and sometimes even lynchings.

At times, individuals as well as organizations have tried to oppose the Klan's terrorist methods. In Illinois and Indiana, a group known as the American Unity League tried to diminish the Klan's power by finding out the identities of Klan members and publishing their names.

However, combating an "invisible" enemy was extremely difficult. Most Klan members remained hooded during raids and strictly adhered to the group's policy of safeguarding one another's anonymity. Secrecy was crucial since known Klan involvement could jeopardize a member's business prospects, his standing in the community, or his chances of being elected to public

African Americans were also hunted and lynched by groups other than the Klan. The Georgia mob in this 1936 photo has lynched 60-year-old Lint Shaw, whom they believed assaulted two young white women and police.

office. Besides being difficult to target and confront, in many areas the Klan was also extremely pervasive and deeply woven into the community's fabric.

The 1920s was an important Klan growth period, as its nationwide membership expanded to between 4 and 5 million individuals.[3] Yet after a time, public ridicule of the Klan's overzealous and often sadistic methods as well as internal dissension among members chipped away at the organization's solidarity. In the 1930s the Klan was once again active only in the South, and by the mid-1940s it dissolved for the second time.

1946 TO PRESENT: A RESURGENCE In 1946 a Georgia physician named Samuel Green breathed new life into the organization. He traveled throughout the country praising white superiority and sponsoring rallies. When he died just three years later the Klan continued, but the organization splintered into separate and often competing Klan groups. Yet the various Klan chapters were still united in their desire for racial purity and their frequent reliance on violent methods to enforce their wishes.

Ku Klux Klan terrorism reached perhaps its zenith in the 1960s in response to that decade's civil rights movement. During that period Klan members were involved in the murder of three civil rights workers in Mississippi as well as in the deaths of four small African-American girls in a Mobile, Alabama, church bombing. Urban unrest among minorities made some more fearful and more open to the Klan's ideas. By 1967 the KKK had reached a post–World War II membership high of 55,000.[4]

However, a subsequent investigation conducted by the House of Representatives's Committee on Un-American Activities revealed both questionable KKK financial dealings as well as documented acts of terrorism. The committee's report, along with the criminal convictions and imprisonment of several Klan leaders, resulted in a marked decline for the organization. By 1981 the Ku Klux Klan had had about 10,000 members, among them extremists who furthered the group's already violent reputation.

Among the headline-making cases was the Klan's intimidation of Vietnamese refugees in Texas who had taken up shrimp fishing in Galveston Bay. After a number of Vietnamese fishermen had become prosperous from fishing in the area, jealous white seamen launched a hate campaign against the newcomers accusing them of overfishing local waters and selling their catches at lower prices to undercut the competition. Determined to drive the Vietnamese Americans from the area, the white fishermen contacted the Klan for assistance.

The Texas Klan eagerly became involved, regarding the fishing dispute as part of a larger international conspiracy among people of color to wrench control of the nation from the white majority. Klansmen were determined to reclaim Galveston Bay as the exclusive territory of the white race. "Enough of this backing up and retreating," one Klan spokesperson said. "Enough of this lip service and no action. It's time to begin to reclaim this country for white people. Now I want you to understand that they're not going to give it to us. If you want it, you're gonna have to get it the way the founding fathers got it—blood! blood! blood! The founding fathers shed their blood to give you this country, and if you want to hold on to it, you're going to have to shed some of yours."[5]

Over the following weeks the Klan began a drive to force the immigrants out. The Klan's first act against the Vietnamese Americans was to paint the words "USS VietCong"—a phrase referring to the Vietnamese rebels Americans fought during the Vietnam War—on a refugee's boat and setting fire to it. The Klan made threats to marina operators who rented dock space to Vietnamese Americans as well as to local businessmen who traded with the newcomers.

Within days, two additional Vietnamese-American ships were set ablaze. Crosses were also burned at the home of a refugee shrimper as well as at the dock where many immigrant fishermen kept their boats. On several evenings, groups of robed Klansmen openly carrying semi-automatic weapons and shotguns patrolled coastal waters.

Whites who befriended the Vietnamese Americans became Klan targets as well. Many found Klan business cards in their mailboxes which read: "You Have Been Paid a Social Visit by the Knights of the Ku Klux Klan. Don't Make the Next Visit a Business Call." Alongside the message was a picture of a hooded Klansman holding a fiery torch while mounted on a galloping horse.

Much of the fervor behind the Klan's anti-refugee activities dissipated, however, following a court injunction banning the group's intimidation tactics. The day after the injunction was issued, the official shrimping season began without incident and those who had been afraid to voice their support for the Vietnamese-American neighbors finally began to do so.

Meanwhile, in other parts of the country the Klan was still at large. In 1981 the Klan murdered a nineteen-year-old African-American student from Mobile, Alabama, named Michael Donald. The crime took place on the night of March 21, as Donald was heading home from his sister's house. Two white men in a vehicle beckoned him over pretending to ask for directions. Moments later he was abducted at gunpoint and driven out to a deserted wooded area where his captors beat him and slit his throat. They then brought his corpse back into town and hung it from a tree.

The Klan members who killed Michael Donald were eventually tried and convicted for his murder. The Klan itself was dealt a further serious blow through a civil suit filed by the victim's mother, Beulah Mae Donald, with the help of the Southern Poverty Law Center. After four hours of deliberating, an all-white jury awarded Ms. Donald a $7-million settlement against the United Klans of America (UKA) and six of its members. The verdict set a precedent for victims of white-supremacist violence by holding the Klan financially liable for the criminal acts of its members. As partial payment of the award, the victim's mother received the deed to the UKA's national headquarters near Tuscaloosa, Alabama—the organization's only substantial asset.

Through the mid 1980s and early 1990s the Klan suffered other legal setbacks resulting in serious financial difficulties for the organization. In 1987 civil rights activists sued the Klan after

Armed Klansmen aboard a shrimp-boat patrol in Galveston Bay in Texas in an attempt to intimidate Vietnamese fishermen. The boat flies the Confederate flag, often used in Klan activities.

its members hurled rocks at demonstrators participating in a march through Forsyth County, Georgia, to commemorate Dr. Martin Luther King, Jr., Day. Finding the Klan guilty of violating the marchers' right to free expression, a U.S. district court in Atlanta awarded the demonstrators $950,400 in damages.

While trying to remain viable despite substantial monetary reverses, the Klan has also suffered from a steady decline in its membership, a decline that was only slowed in 1990. Although organized hate may be flourishing, the Klan has lost numerous potential members to other, more militant organizations. A 1991 survey prepared by Klanwatch, a Klan monitoring group, indicated: "In recent years there has been a falling off in the number of Klan-type groups, as younger people rejected the robes and rituals in favor of paramilitary type groups. . . . The newer groups with 'glamour leaders' (also) attract (more) media attention."[6]

Yet few would characterize the Ku Klux Klan as defunct. In commenting on its effectiveness in the late 1980s, then U.S. Senator Michael Figures noted that the Klan still remains "a force to be watched and not taken for granted."[7] His warning seemed particularly relevant when in April 1992 leaders from one of the Klan's largest orders—The Christian Knights—traveled from their North Carolina headquarters to Long Island, New York, to swear in new members and lay the groundwork for a new group chapter.

The Klan had been active in parts of Long Island during the 1920s, but local law-enforcement officials reported that this was the first time in years that the white-supremacist organization returned to the area. While it is not certain why the Klan targeted Long Island, Tom Halpern, assistant fact-finding director for the Anti-Defamation League, stated that "their usual (motive) is to try to exploit some existing tension." He added: "It seems pretty clear that the (new chapter) is just getting started. . . . At this point, they probably have a very small handful (of recruits). It remains to be seen if it takes hold."[8]

However, the North Carolina Klansmen appeared confident about their Long Island recruitment. Klan leaders declined to disclose the number attending their area initiation ceremony, but stressed that "there are more (members) today than there were yesterday, and there will be more tomorrow than today."[9] In an observation chilling to those wary of hate-group activities, Klan Imperial Wizard Virgil Griffin noted: "We didn't leave North Carolina without a reason—people called us."[10]

THE FUTURE: EXPORTING HATE? An equally disturbing 1990s trend has been the Klan's overseas involvement in white-supremacist movements. Reports of Ku Klux Klan support for Europe's growing neo-Nazi groups are becoming increasingly common.

Grand Dragon Dennis Mahon of the White Knights of the Ku Klux Klan in Tulsa, Oklahoma, has been instrumental in nurturing budding white-supremacist groups on the other side of the Atlantic. In the fall of 1991 Mahon conducted a secret recruitment and propaganda tour through twenty German cities. While abroad, he supplied white supremacists with military manuals containing instructions on manufacturing explosives and detonators. Lessons in guerrilla

German neo-Nazi activity was increasing before the Klan began to export its racist philosophy. In 1987, these neo-Nazis attempted to honor a grave belonging to the family of former Hitler deputy Rudolf Hess.

warfare and sabotage were made available as well. Mahon also claimed that he signed up scores of neo-Nazis as international Klan members, although some believe this to be an exaggeration.

The Grand Dragon has expressed several reasons for his interest in fostering German white supremacy. On numerous occasions, some Klan members have stressed that it might be best to leave the United States if the race situation were to significantly worsen. "As America's turning into a Third World, we may have to go back to our homeland," Mahon remarked speculating about a Klan "return" to Germany. "And I'd like to see Europe stay white and not be overrun. And I'd like to see the German nation get its pride back. I'm sick and tired of these liberals and these Jews telling the German people how bad they are." [11]

The U.S. government can do little to limit Klan race-baiting activities abroad. The First Amendment protects the group's right to publish whatever materials it desires, and the Supreme Court has ruled that the use of the international postal system is a form of free speech. So unless the Klan sends firearms or obscene materials, which it has not, the government's hands are tied.

Yet even though American authorities have been unable to curb Klan involvement in Germany's white-supremacist movement, concerned Berlin officials have launched an inquiry to determine the extent of the Klan's role in neo-Nazi activity. German law-enforcement agents suspect the Klan of having carried out a number of violent acts, since burning crosses and Klan literature have been found at many of the sites of reported racial attacks.

THREE

NEW WHITE SUPREMACY: THE WAVE SPREADS

Throughout the late 1980s and early 1990s, newer white-supremacist organizations have challenged the power and authority of the Ku Klux Klan. Among them are a number of youth-oriented white-power groups known as racist skinheads. While Klan members have traditionally concealed their identities under hoods and robes, racist skinheads are usually identifiable through their shaved heads, steel-toed boots, jeans, and suspenders. Often they travel in groups and have tattoos of Nazi or satanic emblems.

Skinheads originated in Great Britain, where in the early 1990s the group had a following of 8,000 to 10,000 members. Racist skinheads first appeared in the United States in 1984 when a small Chicago group called Romantic Violence began distributing anti-Semitic leaflets and attending hate-group gatherings in Illinois and Michigan. The following year the group's leader was arrested for painting swastikas in a public park. During the early

Taking up the Klan banner: Racist skinheads march against Martin Luther King, Jr., Day in 1989.

1990s it was estimated that there were approximately 3,000 racist skinheads in thirty-four states. Similar skinhead groups also exist in Canada, Australia, New Zealand, Germany, South Africa, Scandinavia, and Latin America.

Not all skinheads are racists. A number of these youths merely adopt the skinhead "look" and enjoy listening to music such as thrash and hardcore rock. These young people maintain a skinhead look and life-style but do not crusade for racial purity. As one nonracist skinhead put it: "Being a skinhead does not mean being a Nazi. I happen to have no hair, a black leather jacket, and army boots, and I get stopped all the time by people trying to preach nonviolence to me. I am a pacifist."[1]

THE SKINHEAD PROFILE

However, a growing number of skinheads are both racist and violent. These youths often mouth white-supremacist rhetoric reminiscent of the Klan's. Some outsiders observe that skinhead groups lack a coherent philosophy. "They spout clichés like characters in a hate comic strip," defense lawyer Jean Francois Csizmadia noted. "But there's nothing behind the words. They haven't the faintest grasp of political or social issues."[2] Few, however, underestimate their power to do harm.

While some skinheads are as young as thirteen and others as old as thirty, most are between sixteen and nineteen years of age. Often these people come from similar backgrounds. Many grow up in broken homes and have a history of alcohol or drug abuse. Skinheads are frequently either poor students or have dropped out of school altogether.

Although many skinheads come from low-income families, quite a few have middle-class or even affluent backgrounds. "Some middle-class youngsters join skinhead organizations as an escapade and later find themselves drawn into the white-power ideology and criminal activity," according to Eva Sears of the Center for Democratic Renewal, who studied the group.[3]

Regardless of their family's financial status, however, the majority of skinheads tend to share the following characteristics:

- No father in the home due to divorce or death.
- Difficulty in getting along with a stepfather when one is present.
- Feelings of powerlessness over life or the future.
- Secondhand exposure to Adolf Hitler's ideology and attraction to the dictator's power over millions of people.

The American Jewish Committee, a watchdog organization that monitors hate-group activities, further reported that "skinhead groups demonstrate an all for one and one for all mentality buttressed by shared lifestyles, uniforms, music, and a dissatisfaction with society at large."[4]

Interviews with the mothers of fascist skinheads revealed that "many (of the youths) . . . have found in the skinheads both a sense of family and a racist philosophy that boosts their self-esteem."[5]

THE SCOPE OF SKINHEAD VIOLENCE Sociologist William Gibson of Southern Methodist University feels that an "element of warrior fantasy" is particularly strong for members of groups like the skinheads.[6] Feeling aban-

Neo-Nazi skinheads in Oregon: According to some, members of racist skinhead groups often seek a sense of purpose and togetherness.

doned or left behind by a society in which minorities are gaining power and prominence, skinheads dream of taking matters into their own hands to return social power to white males.

This philosophy leads racist skinheads throughout the country to frequently assault racial, ethnic, and religious minorities. A gang of Michigan skinheads continually harassed an African-American family that moved into a predominantly white area. At first they stuck white-power stickers on the family's front door and left copies of a racist newsletter on their doorstep. When the family didn't leave town, the violence escalated. On May 19, 1990, a band of drunken skinheads gathered outside the family's home shouting, "We want a piece of your ass, Nigger."[7] A few days later a foot-high cross was burned on the front lawn.

At about the same time a nineteen-year-old skinhead from Casper, Wyoming, admitted shooting at a passing car, claiming that the driver was a member of the Jewish Defense League. His victim was badly wounded in the leg by a bullet that pierced the car door. As it turned out, not only was the skinhead's victim not a member of any organization, he wasn't even Jewish.

In addition to vandalizing community property, Pennsylvania skinheads harassed Jews and gays on a number of occasions. One evening two Pittsburgh-area skinheads pretended to befriend a young homosexual man at a local bar. They later accompanied him home, where the pair robbed the man before kicking him to death with their combat boots.

In 1990 a fortified compound was discovered in Montana which authorities believed might have been a skinhead paramilitary training camp. An Army explosives team inspecting the site uncovered sandbags, foxholes, barbed wire, rifle targets, and chemicals commonly used in manufacturing explosives.[8] It appeared that the group was using the camp to prepare its members for an increase in racist violence.

ALLIES IN HATE While some skinheads already engage in hate crimes, their recent alliances with older, well-established hate groups threaten to escalate racist violence. Some white-supremacist organizations view bonding with the skinheads as a means of energizing their memberships. As early as September 1988, skinheads paraded with neo-Nazis and Ku Klux Klan members in Lawrenceville, Georgia, during the Klan's annual Stone Mountain Rally. Skinheads also attempted to demonstrate with the Klan and other white supremacists during the 1988 Democratic National Convention in Atlanta, but were stopped by the police.

According to many, one of the most dangerous developments in the racist skinhead movement has been its attraction to the beliefs of German Nazism. Although many racist skinheads have appeared to possess no accepted or historically valid understanding of Adolf Hitler and the Nazi movement in Germany prior to World War II, they have often depicted themselves as young American inheritors of a German Nazi creed.

Skinheads have not been the first Americans to describe themselves as Nazis. In 1958 George Lincoln Rockwell founded the American Nazi Party (ANP), also known as the National Socialist White People's Party. Headquartered in Vir-

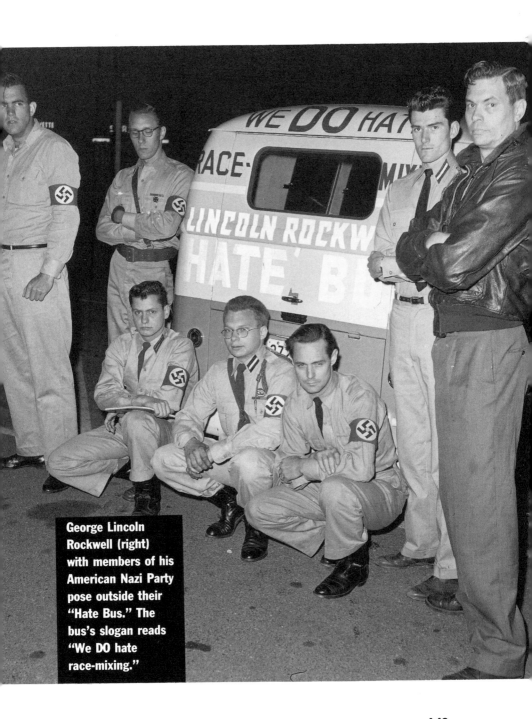

George Lincoln Rockwell (right) with members of his American Nazi Party pose outside their "Hate Bus." The bus's slogan reads "We DO hate race-mixing."

ginia, the ANP practiced military-type drills, wore Nazi uniforms, and dispensed Nazi paraphernalia. The party, however, possessed fewer than forty official members and was poorly organized. In 1967 Rockwell himself was killed by a party member.

W.A.R. Although many have characterized the American Nazi Party as being all but defunct, few have dismissed the skinheads' embrace of Nazism. This is due to the fact that these young, would-be Nazis have aligned themselves with an organization called the White Aryan Resistance (W.A.R.) run by Tom Metzger. Metzger, a middle-aged television repairman from southern California, is the leader of this white-supremacist organization which has claimed to have over five thousand members. A former California Grand Dragon of the Ku Klux Klan, Metzger left the Klan once he felt the group had lost much of its vigor. He and his son John poured their energy into founding W.A.R. and its young people's affiliate, W.A.R. Youth, also known as the Aryan Youth Movement.

Like other white-supremacist organizations, the Metzgers picked up the term *Aryan* in their groups' names from the German Nazis of the 1930s. Like the Nazis, they employed it to describe a superior "master race" of whites whom they believed were destined to rule others.

Hoping to pave the way for this Aryan race— of which they are key members—to ascend to power, the Metzgers have enlisted the help of skinheads, whom they have referred to as their "frontline troops" for battle. To justify acts of racist violence perpetrated by skinheads, Tom

Metzger has frequently characterized their deeds as acts of "self-defense."[9] Attempting to boost skinhead membership, he published the addresses of skinhead groups in Alabama, California, Illinois, Michigan, Oregon, Tennessee, and Wisconsin in W.A.R.'s newsletter. This publication has also tended to glorify individuals perpetrating racially motivated crimes, while it refers to those imprisoned for such deeds as prisoners of war.

Tom Metzger's battle to restore white America to prominence has also focused on the country's nonwhite immigrants. "White people are on their way out unless they do something," he stated. "The worst invasion is the biological invasion. [Immigrants] come here and have children and take over. It's the same in Canada which is allowing masses of people from the Third World into the country."[10] Metzger later publicly announced: "White working class kids have organized for their own self-defense. Violence has worked for the blacks. Every time they threaten violence, they get what they want."[11]

In the fall of 1988 the Metzgers sent San Diego W.A.R. members to Portland, Oregon, to promote white-supremacist violence among members of a skinhead group known as East Side White Pride. These agents encouraged the skinheads to physically attack minorities, and the consequences proved to be deadly.

Late in the evening on November 12, 1988, a group of East Side White Pride skinheads was leaving a friend's home when one of them spied an African-American male at the other end of the block. The man was an Ethiopian immigrant named Mulugeta Seraw, who was saying good-bye to his friends before heading for his apartment. When Seraw's friends tried to drive off, one of the skinheads smashed their car windows with a baseball bat. Then he turned to Seraw and swung the bat in repeated blows to his victim's head. Shortly afterward Mulugeta Seraw lay dead in the street with his skull split open.

When they were later arrested, the skinheads initially claimed that Seraw was killed as they defended themselves against him in a street fight. But after several witnesses came forward with a radically different story, the bat-wielding skinhead pleaded guilty to murder and was sentenced to thirty years to life in prison. Two of his accomplices pleaded guilty to manslaughter and were imprisoned as well.

Law-enforcement officials had previously linked the Metzgers to racially motivated violence and vandalism. A Tom Metzger disciple committed murder in Nevada, while a number of his California followers had busied themselves defacing synagogues. Yet in these instances and others, Metzger was not held accountable for the destructive results of his rhetoric and support.

In the Seraw case, however, two civil rights groups, the Anti-Defamation League and the Southern Poverty Law Center, devised a unique strategy to make Metzger pay for Seraw's murder. They decided to sue the Metzgers in civil court for monetary damages. Civil rights attorney Morris Dees explained the dual purpose of the suit: "I feel that this was an opportunity to not only gain money for (Seraw's family), but to put Metzger, who has the most violent, the most dangerous white-supremacist group operating in America today, out of business."[12]

Dees's goal was to destroy W.A.R.'s power base by financially crippling the Metzgers and their organization. He hoped to invoke the principle of "vicarious liability," arguing that the organization should pay substantial monetary penalties for indirectly inciting the violence that led to Seraw's murder. Dees was aware of the difficult challenge he faced, since he had to directly link Metzger to Seraw's murder, which had taken place more than 1,500 miles from W.A.R. headquarters.

Metzger's courtroom opponents were fortunate in having Dave Mazzella, one of W.A.R.'s lieutenants sent to Portland to organize the skinheads, testify against the group's extremist leader. The crucial link between Metzger and Seraw's murder proved to be a letter from W.A.R. introducing Mazzella to East Side White Pride's leadership. In court, Mazzella revealed that while Tom Metzger had sent numerous W.A.R. lieutenants like himself to Oklahoma, Florida, Texas, and other areas to incite skinhead violence, Metzger had been particularly effective in using Mazzella to spur on the Oregon youths.

Mazzella testified that on the night of the murder he and the skinheads passed out Metzger's racist flyers in downtown Portland. Following a meeting later that evening, the group even drew a picture of an African American with a bullet through his head.

These incidents convinced the jury that Tom Metzger, his son, and their associates were responsible for encouraging the violence leading

Dave Mazzella, center, with two W.A.R. skinheads.

Tom Metzger (left) and his son John in 1990 just after their white power groups were linked to Mulugeta Seraw's murder.

to Seraw's death. Tom Metzger was ordered to pay $5 million in damages, his son $1 million, and his organization W.A.R. $3 million. To satisfy the court award, Metzger had to sell his home and W.A.R.'s printing presses. Furthermore, a portion of any income he was to receive in the future was to go to Seraw's family, according to the sentence.

THE IDENTITY CHURCH The Klan's recent setbacks and W.A.R.'s financial troubles have not, however, collapsed America's growing white-power movement. Many other active groups have embraced the racist principles associated with the Identity Church. This quasi-religious organization holds that white Anglo-Saxons are descended from the Ten Lost Tribes of biblical times. The Ten Lost Tribes were traditionally thought to be ten of the original twelve Hebrew tribes that formed the independent kingdom of Israel in 930 B.C. Not only has the Identity Church characterized these tribes as Anglo-Saxon, but it claims they—and not Jews—are the "chosen people." The church further asserts that Jesus Christ was not a Jew but was instead the true ancestor of the white northern European peoples. Movement followers regard African Americans and other nonwhites as "mud people" who lack souls and are spiritually equivalent to animals. Although the Identity Church rationale was initially seized on by U.S. white supremacists during the late 1970s and early 1980s, its roots in the United States extend back to the 1940s and to nineteenth-century Britain.

Hostility and even violence toward nonwhites and Jews are basic to Identity Church beliefs. Some Identity followers contend that the United

States will ultimately experience a cataclysmic race war, and they are already preparing for this bloody encounter.

Among the groups which embody Identity principles is the Aryan Nations. Based in Idaho's panhandle, this neo-Nazi group claims to represent the "real" America, as it offers followers a unique blend of bigotry and biblical interpretation. The group's founder and leader is Reverend Richard Butler, pastor of the Church of Jesus Christ Christian—a religious sect that espouses Identity principles and infuses racism into religious teachings.

Butler is not a newcomer to white-supremacist activism. As early as 1976, law-enforcement authorities discovered a well-concealed bunker in the southern California desert containing over five tons of illegal arms and ammunition. The contraband included machine guns, mortars, land mines, and even napalm. Their investigation connected the bunker to a white-supremacist group known as the Christian Defense League headed by Richard Butler, though he could not be directly linked to the arms stash.

Butler and a number of his followers then relocated to a twenty-acre stretch of wooded land near Hayden Lake, Idaho, where they formed the Aryan Nations. The new group's purpose, as described by Reverend Butler, was to remain racially separate: "We are talking about creating a national state for the white Aryan, the only people upon the face of the earth that does not have a national state."[13]

Utilizing both his organization and church, Butler created a high-volume propaganda network to spread his message through press re-

Richard Butler in front of a stained-glass window in one of his Identity "churches."

leases, newsletters, pamphlets, and taped sermons. The Aryan Nations also operates a small school for the children of Idaho members, where students learn the 4 R's—reading, 'riting, 'rithmetic, and racism.

Like Tom Metzger's W.A.R., the Aryan Nations has reached out to other organizations to form broad-based white-supremacist affiliations. International congresses held at Hayden Lake drew followers of more than a dozen white-supremacist groups. In addition, toward the close of 1987, Richard Butler began extending his organization's activities into Utah.

IDENTITY BEHIND BARS

Among the Aryan Nations' many activities was an intensive recruitment drive at various penitentiaries. They circulated flyers among inmates and urged convicts to join them in Idaho following their releases. Many prison inmates were attracted to white-supremacist ideology because they already bore grudges against society and the legal system and felt that they had little left to lose.

The Aryan Brotherhood, a white-supremacist prison organization, had strong ties to the Aryan Nations. According to the U.S. Justice Department, the Brotherhood has existed in federal and state prisons in Arizona, Arkansas, California, Kentucky, Missouri, Ohio, and Oklahoma. A similar gang, known as the Aryan Warriors, has been active within the Nevada prison system.

Prisoners who join white-supremacist gangs often become involved in the "churches" created by racist organizations and then attempt to claim the same privileges enjoyed by inmates belonging to conventional religions. Prisoners who joined the Aryan Nations through Richard Butler's Church of Jesus Christ Christian have demanded the right to receive organizational literature, hold white-supremacist "church services," and be visited by church "pastors."

The Aryan Nations, as well as other white-supremacist organizations, sometimes provide legal assistance to prisoners. It encourages them to make all complaints regarding violations of their "white rights" in writing, file formal administrative complaints with the prison warden when necessary, insist on equal rights with minority inmates, and file any civil rights complaints in federal courts. White-supremacist groups have encouraged entering the U.S. legal system only as a last resort, however, because they believe it is controlled by Jews, whom they refer to collectively as "ZOG, or the Zionist Occupational Government." [14]

Even though prisoners are technically permitted to pursue the religion of their choice, in 1984 the Religious Advisory Council of the Idaho Department of Corrections debated whether this rule pertains to the Aryan Nations' Church of Jesus Christ Christian. After reviewing the data, the council determined that prisoners may join any religious faction that promotes genuine religious concepts, but not ones that foster hatred, violence, and the overthrow of the U.S. government.

Idaho prisoners were subsequently denied access to Butler's religious teachings due to what the council termed its "open advocacy of violence, mayhem, and murder." [15] As the council stated: "Mr. Butler would have us believe that Aryans have the right *and* obligation to kill anyone who is not white, whether or not they have robbed anyone and whether or not they present a danger to the 'preservation' of anyone. In short, Mr. Butler is calling for all peoples of the white race to rise up and kill all nonwhites.''[16]

Even though Aryan Nations propaganda has been banned, these materials are still frequently smuggled into correctional institutions. Although white-supremacist attorneys have legally challenged the right of the correctional system to withhold the inflammatory literature, they have so far been unsuccessful.

TARGET: THOSE WHO DISAGREE In the fall of 1983 an ultra–right wing band of Aryan Nations followers formed a new violence-prone group known as the Order. The group has also gone by the names Bruder Schweigen or Silent Brotherhood (which differs from the Bruder Schweigen Strike Force Two), the White American Bastion, and the Aryan Resistance Movement. Its ultimate goal was to establish a separate Aryan homeland in the U.S. Pacific Northwest which would function independently of the United States government. To finance the plan, in 1983 and 1984 the group conducted a series of armored-car robberies that netted over $4.5 million for their cause. The Order's other criminal activities included counterfeiting U.S. currency, arson, shoot-outs with FBI agents, and the murder of Jewish radio personality Alan Berg.

Berg, who had been a harsh critic of white supremacy, was what was meant to be the first target in a string of assassinations by the Order. Barry Kowalski, deputy chief of the Justice Department's Criminal Section, described the group's intent: ''The plan was to assassinate primarily Jewish leaders and send a shock wave out to the country."[17] His assessment of the group was confirmed by the Order's Declaration of War, signed by thirteen of its members on November 25, 1984. It reads:

We from this day forward declare that we no longer consider the regime in Washington to be a valid and lawful representative of all Aryans who refuse to submit to the coercion and subtle tyranny placed upon us by Tel Aviv (Israel) and their lackeys in Washington. . . . Let friend and foe alike be made aware. This is war![18]

The group's statement further warned that some U.S. congressmen might be lynched and that numerous federal agents, police officers, armed forces enlistees, bankers, judges, journalists, and business representatives were considered suitable murder targets as well.

Prompt FBI intervention, combined with the efforts of local law-enforcement officials, was instrumental in effectively reining in the Order's violent crime spree. Eventually more than two dozen Order members were arrested in thirteen states. The majority of those who signed the Declaration of War and participated in the organization's criminal activities eventually ended up serving lengthy federal prison terms.

CSA AND OTHER IDENTITY SECTS Founded in 1971, the Covenant, the Sword, and the Arm of The Lord (CSA) is another violent white-supremacist group whose activities have been curtailed by effective law enforcement. Operating for the most part out of a secluded communal settlement located on 224 acres of land near the Arkansas-Missouri border, the men, women, and children that constituted its following at its peak believed that America was near collapse and would eventually be engaged in a disastrous race war.

In preparation, CSA members stored away food and medicine and stockpiled an enormous assortment of arms and munitions, some of which were made on the compound. Members also regularly participated in wilderness survival exercises and paramilitary training sessions. CSA's Identity Church doctrine teaches that "Jews are the seed of Satan, not the seed of God." Kerry Noble, one of the group's elders and church ministers, described their followers as "Christian survivalists who believe in preparing for the ultimate holocaust." [19] Prosecution of the group for a series of crimes including the firebombing of an Indiana synagogue, the arson of a Missouri church, and the illegal manufacture of weapons resulted in CSA's virtual dissolution.

The Posse Comitatus, which was organized in 1969, consists of loosely knit gangs of armed vigilantes and survivalists who worship at their own Identity-based churches. In Latin the words *posse comitatus* mean "power of the county" and, as its name suggests, group members fervently believe in local government. They are highly suspicious of state and federal officials, whom they feel are often little more than paid puppets of Jews and other perceived enemies of the white race. Some Posse Comitatus members have even refused to pay federal taxes.

At one time the Posse Comitatus was active

in at least thirteen states, but this number has varied as successful law-enforcement efforts have at times closed down the group's operations in some states. The organization gained national notoriety in 1983 when one of its members, Gordon Kahl, killed two federal marshals in a North Dakota shootout and was subsequently forced into hiding. The marshals had been after Kahl for both a probation violation and non-payment of taxes. Kahl died later on in an encounter with Arkansas lawmen. Following his death, he became a martyr to the white-supremacist movement.

Numerous other Identity-based sects exist besides those discussed here. Even though many have small memberships, their destructive potential can often be significant. This is especially true when white-supremacist groups pool resources to strengthen their impact. Their determination to thrive despite the odds against them is intense. As white-supremacist leader Tom Metzger put it: "They knock one of us down and a thousand more stand up."[20]

FOUR

SANITIZING WHITE SUPREMACY

While some groups and individuals in today's white-power movement favor militant and extremist tactics, others have chosen a different course to advance their philosophy. They advocate toning down offensive racist rhetoric and violence to make their organizations and beliefs more acceptable to mainstream America.

Many observers speculate that rather than changing out of a true desire to become less racist, these groups and their leaders are just seeking to avoid costly lawsuits such as the one in which Tom Metzger was held personally liable for his organization's deeds. At secret meetings that took place in Arkansas and North Carolina during the early 1990s, two of the nation's largest Klan groups agreed to encourage rank-and-file members to be less outspoken regarding the groups' ultra–right wing views on race. Klan leaders also disagreed about the strong affiliations some chapters have developed with violent skinheads. While several Klan representatives felt this bond was an excellent recruiting tool, others thought such associations could eventually result in the Klan's downfall.

Although the topic remains hotly debated in some white-power circles, a number of Klan groups have already gone out of their way to clean up their organization's unwholesome image. They have, however, not always been entirely successful, as Reidville, North Carolina, Klan members learned after they eagerly offered their services in the state's "Adopt-a-Highway" program. Through this undertaking over 5,000 civic and social organizations pledged to keep 10,000 miles of North Carolina's highways litter-free. The Klan had hoped to maintain 3 miles of U.S. Highway 158 and in return wanted a sign noting its civic contribution posted along the roadside. But North Carolina's Department of Transportation turned down the Klan's offer, arguing that the organization was "atypical" of the groups that were involved in the program.

DAVID DUKE Other white supremacists have managed to effectively revamp their public images. Perhaps the man best known for doing so is former Ku Klux Klan Grand Wizard David Duke. Duke's contempt for people of other races surfaced early in his life, and some believe it might have been an outgrowth of his turbulent teen years. His sister's teenage marriage made him the only child in a troubled household at the age of twelve. Four years later his father left home taking a U.S. State Department engineering position in the Southeast Asian country of Laos.

Duke remained home alone with his alcoholic mother who went in and out of various hospital treatment programs. He was so angered and frustrated by his mother's inability to conquer her addiction that their housekeeper claimed he once threatened to cover his mother with hairspray and set her on fire.

When preparing a school term-paper exploring the downside of integration, the teenage Duke visited the offices of a segregationist group known as the White Citizen's Council. There he found willing male mentors who served as father figures while introducing him to Klan and Nazi doctrines.

David Duke openly displayed his zeal for white power at John F. Kennedy High School, often successfully intimidating those around him. "In twenty-eight years of teaching, he was the only student I was afraid of," recalled retired high-school social studies teacher Leola M. Williams.[1] When Duke arrived at Louisiana State University in the fall of 1968, his obsession with Nazism and Aryan superiority intensified. Donning Nazi apparel, he tried to convert fellow students to fascist philosophy, causing him to be ridiculed by some and regarded as seriously disturbed by others. Graduate assistant Beth Courtney remembered that Duke frequently insisted on debating Nazi principles with members of the university's history department. "He would argue that history didn't take place the way we were teaching it," she said.[2] She further noted that Duke barely passed the course she taught.

As David Duke grew older, he realized that he might be more successful if he softened his

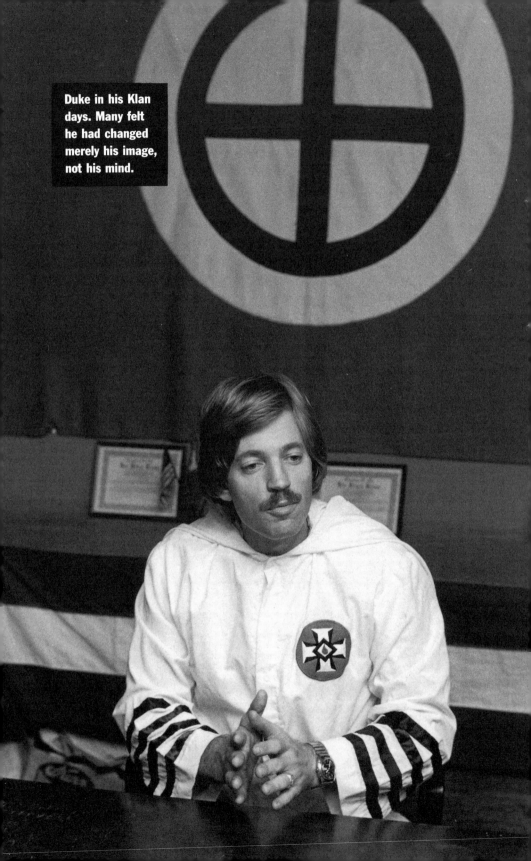

Duke in his Klan days. Many felt he had changed merely his image, not his mind.

extremist approach and adopted a more middle-of-the road image. He shelved his nearly fanatical devotion to Nazism to emerge as a somewhat charismatic and photogenic Klan Grand Wizard who made frequent television appearances. Duke wanted to redefine the Klan as an organization capable of attracting bright, personable whites and hoped to trade the group's traditional hooded robes for three-piece suits. He was even credited by I. A. Botnick of the Anti-Defamation of New Orleans with bringing "the Klan out of the cow pasture and into hotel meeting rooms."[3]

David Duke left the Knights of the Ku Klux Klan in 1980, but retained links to the racist right. Eager to launch his own political career, Duke founded the National Association for the Advancement of White People, basing the organization's name on the civil rights organization the National Association for the Advancement of Colored People. Although he was already generally regarded as physically attractive, Duke underwent a significant amount of cosmetic surgery to enhance his appearance. Some felt these changes were aimed at achieving an image associated with the term Aryan—blond hair, blue eyes, and physical strength.

Duke made political gains in 1989 after being elected to the Louisiana House of Representatives from the largely white New Orleans suburb of Metairie. Following this important career move, Duke tried to broaden his popular appeal, claiming that after truly finding God, he had thrown off the racial hatred that had once dominated his life. As he continued his quest for political power, Duke asked voters to forget his past and concentrate on his new message of lower taxes and less government. "If you can get away from the rhetoric and the smear tactics," Duke said, referring to negative press about his racist past, "you'll find you agree with me."[4]

Yet many doubted that Duke had undergone a genuine metamorphosis. The question of Duke's sincerity became paramount in the fall of 1991 when he finished second in an unusual open primary election in Louisiana. He then became the Republican party's nominee for governor of the state, despite the party's disavowal of him.

Although Duke consistently tried to repudiate his racist past in his bid for the governorship, his record revealed a different picture. While in 1991 Duke claimed to "respect the Jewish people,"[5] just a few years earlier—following his supposed Christian conversion—Duke was quoted as saying: "(Jews) probably deserve to go into the ash bin of history."[6] As late as 1989 his organization also sold racist music including a song entitled "Niggers Never Die."[7]

The situation worsened for Duke when a campaign aide left during the governor's race, claiming that the candidate's newfound Christianity had been a sham. The aide reported that during an August parade prior to the November 1991 election, Duke cursed a group of young African Americans who threw mud at his vehicle. The Republican gubernatorial candidate is alleged to have also said, "Those niggers went crazy."[8]

In the end, Duke lost the election to the Democratic candidate. The record turnout of African-American voters and people's fear of economically harming the state by electing a candidate from America's racist fringe were cited as factors in his downfall. As one comedian joked re-

After repudiating his racist past, former Klan Grand Wizard David Duke ran as the Republican candidate for governor of Louisiana. The Republican party then repudiated him.

garding the former neo-Nazi's potential effect on the tourist trade: "What can Duke do? Build hotels for an influx of elderly German travelers?"

Yet many feel that David Duke's participation in American politics cannot be scoffed at. His sanitized appearance and mainstreamed message allowed him to garner a majority of the white vote. Duke's growing appeal was further confirmed by the fact that over 40 percent of his $1.37 million dollars in campaign contributions came from supporters in 46 states.

To his opponents' disappointment, the Louisiana setback has not daunted Duke's political aspirations. He successfully used the publicity generated by his candidacy to expand the national forum for his racist political agenda. In 1992 David Duke made a bid for the Republican party's presidential nomination though he did not receive the same level of support he had received in Louisiana's elections. In assessing his recent defeats, Duke told his followers that this was just "the beginning, not the end,"[9] and few doubted in the early 1990s that American politics had not heard the last of David Duke.

THE DUKE LEGACY

In fact, many predicted an increase of young, racist would-be politicians molded in David Duke's image. Shortly after Duke's gubernatorial defeat, Thom Robb, who assumed the post of Grand Wizard in Duke's old Klan group in 1989, announced his plans to operate a high-tech training facility for white supremacists who wish to follow Duke into American politics. "Louisiana has one David Duke," Robb noted. "We plan to give America a thousand of them."[10]

The idea behind the new strategy was to substitute racist rhetoric and violence with well-packaged conservative campaigns against affirmative action policies and hiring quotas that aid minorities, welfare programs, and funding for AIDS research. Robb promised that potential political leaders spawned from the Klan "will be taught to avoid statements that sound hateful and turn people off."[11] He proposed seminars on public "imaging," which would include advising candidates on how to come off well in televised interviews. He noted that more attention would be paid to grooming, fashion, and hygiene. "They always have these pictures of people in the Klan, flies buzzing around the head, teeth missing, and wiping manure off their feet. If you're a person who wants to take some kind of leadership position and you've got bad teeth, (you've got to) get your teeth fixed," Robb added.[12]

But even though Robb's re-packaging of white supremacy was aimed at altering the movement's look, few doubted that his philosophy had changed. Robb said he has attempted not to use the term "nigger," although he admitted to often slipping back into old habits.[13] Robb and his followers have also maintained the belief that the federal government has been hampered by strong Jewish influences. They have also advocated the eventual separation of the races. He has frequently stressed that, "from my perspective, America is a white nation."[14]

FIVE

WHITE POWER: THE NEXT WAVE

Incidents of racist violence by individuals and organized white supremacists continue today, perhaps even as you read this book. Yet while reports of these incidents often emerge and disgust us, we frequently dismiss them as the misguided actions of a crazed radical fringe.

But can we afford to continue to do so? In a nationwide 1990 Louis Harris and Associates poll, a majority of U.S. high-school students revealed that if they witnessed a racial attack, they would either assist the assailant or do nothing to stop the assault, since they would assume the violence was justified.[1] In assessing the survey, some social analysts concluded that American young people are becoming increasingly comfortable with bigotry and hatred.

How has racism grown to become more acceptable? We have already seen that racism has deep roots in the history of modern civilization. In addi-

According to many, racism is learned behavior and begins when people are made comfortable with racist and prejudicial ideas at an early age.

tion, economic tensions have frequently been cited as a factor in America's continuing racial problems. As attorney Morris Dees stated: "Many of the jobs that blacks, Hispanics, and Asians are landing used to be reserved for whites alone. Junior, after graduating from high school in Wheeling, West Virginia, used to be certain that a job was waiting for him at the steel mill where his Dad and uncles had worked for the last thirty years. But with fair employment practices, jobs for whites just aren't guaranteed like they used to be. Blacks are actually attaining some of the rights they fought for during the civil rights movement, and many whites are resentful." [2]

Some observers have alleged that the Republican administrations of Ronald Reagan and George Bush contributed to an atmosphere of racism and intolerance. These critics have said that both presidents failed to adequately enforce existing civil rights laws and weakened newly proposed legislation that was intended to achieve greater equality between races. Roger Wilkens, a senior fellow at the Institute for Policy Studies in Washington, D.C., charged that the Reagan administration "in hundreds of ways, . . . said: 'Blacks have gotten too much. We are going to weaken the civil rights enforcement law.' " [3]

Others, however, have disputed these allegations and criticisms. They point out that the Justice Department, under the presidencies of both Ronald Reagan and George Bush, prosecuted such hate groups as the KKK, the Order, and several racist skinheads for criminal activities.

What else can explain the spread of racial hatred? Many social critics believe that racism is perpetuated by people's lack of exposure to diverse cultures. While this is often true for people of all ages, some educators stress that today many youths lack any real knowledge of different groups' past struggles for justice and equality. "They don't know about gas chambers (of the Holocaust) and sit-ins (of the 1960s)," noted Allan Ostar, president of the American Association of State Colleges and Universities.[4]

Some also point to the growing number of white college student unions as an example of growing racism among the young. Members of these groups argue that white students have been deprived of their slice of the American pie and often protest financial aid practices and fair-hiring employment policies which they perceive as detrimental to their race.

The problem escalates when racial hatred and even violence are used as vehicles to either rebel against authority or gain peer acceptance and approval. Jeffrey Ross, Anti-Defamation League director of campus affairs, succinctly described a disturbing trend at some colleges and universities: "Hatred is hip."[5]

White-supremacist groups rely on ignorance and fear to exploit potentially explosive racial situations. To that end they've tried to strategically place their members in mainstream society for maximum effectiveness. "We're embedded now," White Aryan Resistance leader Tom Metzger asserted, describing the movement's pervasiveness. "We're in your colleges, we're in your armies, we're in your police forces. We're in your technical area. We're in your banks. Why do you think a lot of these skinheads have disappeared? 'Cause they grew their hair out and

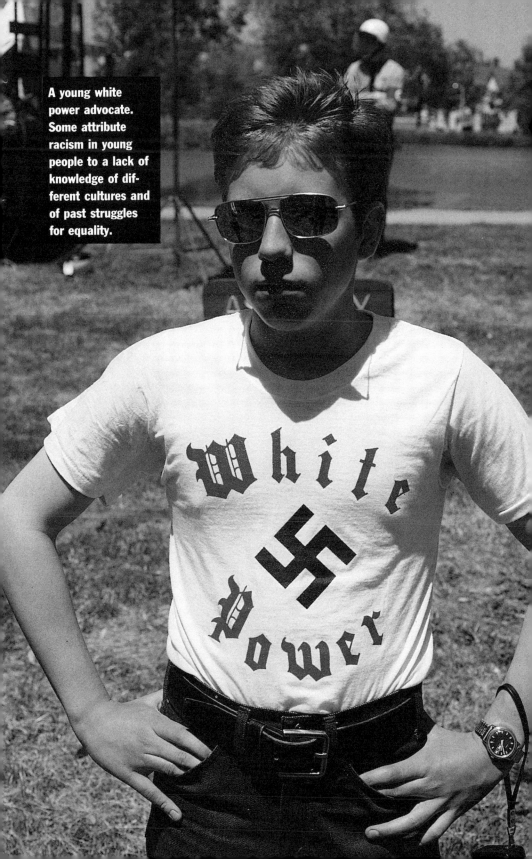

A young white power advocate. Some attribute racism in young people to a lack of knowledge of different cultures and of past struggles for equality.

went to college. They're going. They've got the program. We planted the seeds."[6]

Sociologists stress that people are most vulnerable to racist propaganda during difficult periods in their lives when they feel alienated from the values and belief systems that were once important to them. These individuals are often susceptible to the influences of a charismatic white-supremacist leader who reaches out to them. Professor Robert Lifton of John Jay College of the City University of New York described the process: "You get that kind of interconnection between the primary haters and ordinary people who themselves feel victimized and are hungry for a scapegoat. It can be very frequently economic duress, but it can also be some degree of social fragmentation, or the loss of family stability, job stability, communal stability, all interacting social and economic factors."[7]

PULLING THE PLUG ON WHITE POWER

While there is no simple way to dissipate a growing white-power movement in a free society, various steps may be taken to curb its potentially destructive consequences. In many parts of the country, educators have promoted programs for children that encourage a healthy respect for people of diverse races and religions. Ideally, this "tolerance-oriented" curriculum would continue through secondary school and college, featuring required courses aimed at achieving racial harmony. The Anti-Defamation League along with other organizations monitoring white-supremacist activities have firmly stated that "confronting and eliminating prejudice should be an educational priority at all levels of education."[8]

Keeping a watchful eye on hate groups and designing legislation to limit racist acts are important as well. In 1990 the Hate Crimes Statistics Act was signed into law. The legislation requires the federal government to maintain data on acts of violence motivated by racial, ethnic, and religious hatred. It was generally regarded as a first step in bringing hate crimes to the public's attention, while encouraging more prosecutions and stiffer sentences.

Perhaps equally important are the various seminars and conferences that bring together community members, public officials, law-enforcement authorities, educators, and religious leaders to combat this problem. Diminishing racism and the influence of white-power groups frequently requires both a strong individual commitment to the cause and a willingness to pool resources and work together.

How much we fight against racism depends on the kind of world we want to live in and how far we are willing to go to achieve it. It may mean consistently recognizing and rejecting stereotypes about people whose race or culture differs from our own. It may also entail having the courage to sometimes take an unpopular stand in order to be true to our beliefs. Father Theodore Hesburgh described the challenge this way:

Prejudice is about the easiest sin to come by in any country on earth, including America, and we're all guilty of it from time to time. We don't judge people by their inner spirit or beauty or humanity or goodness; we judge them because they have a different skin color or they may have some

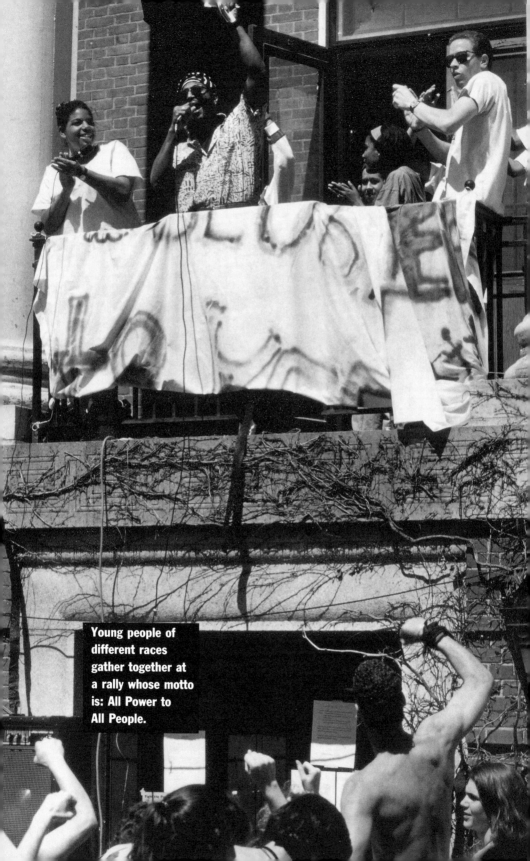

Young people of different races gather together at a rally whose motto is: All Power to All People.

other characteristics, like their hair or their speech or their language or their background. I just think that every so often we've got to go back to those very fundamental things that make this nation strong and make it beautiful, and that is what every young- ster says in school every day—one nation under God with liberty and justice for all.[9]

Whether or not America ever comes close to achieving this ideal partly depends on you and your ultimate rejection of prejudice and racism.

NOTES

CHAPTER ONE
1. Bill Stanton, *Klanwatch: Bringing the Ku Klux Klan to Justice* (New York: Grove Weidenfeld, 1991), p. 8.
2. *Ibid.*
3. Ginny Carroll, "Coming Soon: Klub/KKK," *Newsweek* 118 (July 8, 1991): 30.
4. Anti-Defamation League of B'nai B'rith, *Shaved for Battle: Skinheads Target America's Youth* (New York: Anti-Defamation League, 1987), p. 5.
5. Kenneth S. Stern, *Skinheads: Who They Are & What to Do When They Come to Town* (New York: The American Jewish Committee, 1990), p. 7.
6. Stephen Miller, "Hi-Tech Racism," *Black Enterprise* 18 (October 1987): 22.
7. Chris Lutz, editor, *They All Don't Wear Sheets: A Chronology of Racist and Far-Right Violence* (New York: National Council of the Churches of Christ in the United States, 1987), p. 6.
8. *Ibid.*

CHAPTER TWO
1. Kathleen M. Blee, *Women of the Klan: Racism and Gender in the 1920s* (Berkeley: University of California Press, 1991), p. 83.
2. *Ibid.*
3. Anti-Defamation League of B'nai B'rith, *Hate Groups in America: A Record of Bigotry and Violence* (New York: Anti-Defamation League, 1988), p. 78.
4. *Ibid.*, p. 83.
5. Bill Stanton, *Klanwatch: Bringing the Ku Klux Klan to Justice* (New York: Grove Weidenfeld, 1991), p. 93.
6. Ronald Smothers, "Hate Groups Seen Growing as Neo-Nazis Draw Young," *The New York Times* (February 19, 1992): A13.

7. Marilyn Marshall, "Beulah Mae Donald: The Black Woman Who Beat the Ku Klux Klan," *Ebony* 43 (March 1988): 148.

8. Tom Nolan, "Ku Klux Klan Recruiting in the Hamptons," *New York Post* (April 6, 1992): 7.

9. *Ibid.*

10. *Ibid.*

11. "The Fourth Reich," ABC News *Primetime Live* (January 2, 1992).

CHAPTER THREE

1. Barry Came, "A Growing Menace: Violent Skinheads Are Raising Urban Fears." *MacLeans* 102 (January 23, 1989): 44.

2. *Ibid.*

3. Eva Sears, "Skinheads: A New Generation of Hate Mongers," *USA Today* 117 (May 1989): 24.

4. Kenneth S. Stern, *Skinheads: Who They Are & What to Do When They Come to Town* (New York: The American Jewish Committee, 1990), p. 5.

5. Eva Sears, p. 26.

6. John Leo, "A Chilling Wave of Racism," *Time* (January 25, 1988): 57.

7. Anti-Defamation League of B'nai B'rith, *Neo-Nazi Skinheads: A 1990 Status Report* (New York: Anti-Defamation League, 1990), p. 15.

8. *Ibid.*

9. "Beyond Hate With Bill Moyers," Public Affairs Television (May 19, 1991).

10. Anti-Defamation League of B'nai B'rith, *Special Edition: A Periodic Update from ADL's Civil Rights Division— Tom Metzger* (New York: Anti-Defamation League, 1989), p. 1.

11. Barry Came, p. 43.

12. "Pulling the Strings of Hate," ABC News *20/20* (January 11, 1991).

13. "Bibles and Bigotry," ABC News *Nightline* (September 23, 1983).

14. Anti-Defamation League of B'nai B'rith, *Hate Groups in America: A Record of Bigotry and Violence* (New York: Anti-Defamation League of B'nai B'rith, 1988), p. 58.

15. *Ibid.*

16. *Ibid.*

17. Eloise Salholz, "Curbing the Hate Mongers," *Newsweek* 112 (September 19, 1988): 29.

18. *Ibid.*

19. Anti-Defamation League, *Hate Groups,* p. 44.

20. "Avowed Racist Defiant After Sentencing," *New York Post* (January 4, 1991): 9.

CHAPTER FOUR

1. Bill Turque, "The Real David Duke," *Newsweek* 118 (November 18, 1991): 26.

2. *Ibid.*

3. Carol Stickland, "Clean Sheets for the Klan," *Commonwealth* (February 23, 1990): 102.

4. Bill Turque, p. 24.

5. *Ibid.*

6. Bill Turque, p. 25.

7. *Ibid.*

8. Bill Turque, "Saying No to David Duke," *Newsweek* 118 (November 18, 1991): 19.

9. "A Lesser Evil," *The Star Ledger* (November 19, 1991): 24.

10. "Duke's Old Klan Will Train a Thousand Clones," *The Star Ledger* (November 17, 1991): 1.

11. *Ibid.*

12. Michael Riley, "White & Wrong; New Klan, Old Hatred," *Time* 140 (July 6, 1992): 26.

13. *Ibid.*

14. *Ibid.*

CHAPTER FIVE

1. Keith Geiger, "One Nation Still Imperfect," *NEA Today* 9 (December, 1990): 2.

2. "Racism, Shall We Overcome?" *U.S. Catholic* 55 (December 1990): 30.

3. "Black Leaders in Uproar Over New Surge in Racism," *Jet* 71 (January 6, 1987): 6.

4. Art Levine, "America's Youthful Bigots," *U.S. News & World Report* 108 (May 7, 1990): 60.

5. *Ibid.*

6. "Beyond Hate With Bill Moyers," Public Affairs Television (May 19, 1991).

7. *Ibid.*

8. Anti-Defamation League of B'nai B'rith, 1991 Audit of Anti-Semitic Incidents (New York: Anti-Defamation League, 1992), p. 26.

9. "Bibles and Bigotry," ABC News *Nightline* (September 23, 1983).

FURTHER READING

BOOKS   Blee, Kathleen M. *Women in the Klan: Racism and Gender in the 1920s.* Berkeley: University of California Press, 1991.

Cook, Fred J. *The Ku Klux Klan: America's Recurring Nightmare.* New York: Julian Messner, 1989.

Corcoran, James. *Bitter Harvest: Gordon Kahl & The Posse Comitatus.* New York: Viking Penguin, 1991.

Katz, William L. *The Invisible Empire: Ku Klux Klan Impact on History.* Seattle, Washington: Open Hand, 1986.

Kovel, Joel. *White Racism.* New York: Columbia University Press, 1984.

Kronenwetter, Michael. *United They Hate: White Supremacists in America.* New York: Walker, 1992.

Lang, Susan. *Extremist Groups.* New York: Franklin Watts, 1990.

Leone, Bruno, ed. *Racism: Opposing Viewpoints.* St. Paul, Minnesota: Greenhaven Press, 1986.

Martinez, Thomas, with John Gunther. *Brotherhood of Murder.* New York: McGraw-Hill, 1988.

McKissack, Patricia. *Taking a Stand Against Racism & Racial Discrimination.* New York: Franklin Watts, 1990.

Tarrants, Thomas A., III. *The Conversion of a Klansman: The Story of a Former Ku Klux Klan Terrorist.* Garden City, New York: Doubleday & Company, Inc., 1979.

Thompson, Jerry. *My Life in the Klan.* New York: G. P. Putnam's Sons, 1982.

ARTICLES Church, George J., "Surge to the Right," *Time* 139, January 13, 1992, p. 22.

Cockburn, Alexander, "Dangerous Diversions," *The Nation* 252, May 27, 1991, p. 690.

"Dark Fears," *The Economist* 318, January 12, 1991, p. 22.

Herlinger, Chris, "Getting Harsh with Hate," *Scholastic Update* 124, April 3, 1992, p. 13.

MacKenzie, Hilary, "The Racist Underside: Violence and Insults Inflame Ethnic Discord," *MacLeans* 103, June 25, 1990, p. 80.

Nash, Peter, "Giants in the Land; African Americans' Exodus out of Memory," *The Christian Century* 108, April 3, 1991, p. 373.

Nicholas, Len M., "The New Racism: A Product of Economic Inequality," *USA Today* 119, November 1990, p. 54.

Pilger, John, "Play the White Man's Tune: Black People Fare Worse in Australia Than South Africa," *New Statesman & Society* 5, March 13, 1992, p. 10.

Strickland, William, "Taking Our Souls?," *Essence* 22, November 1991, p. 48.

ORGANIZATIONS CONCERNED WITH RACISM AND DISCRIMINATION

American-Arab Anti-Discrimination Committee
4201 Connecticut Avenue, Suite 500
Washington, D.C. 20008

American Coordinating Committee
for Equality in Sport and Society
c/o Center for Study of Sport
360 Huntington Avenue
Boston, MA 02215

American Jewish Committee
165 East 56th Street
New York, NY 10022

Anti-Defamation League of B'nai B'rith
823 United Nations Plaza
New York, NY 10017

Anti-Repression Resource Team
P.O. Box 122
Jackson, MS 39205

Asian American Legal Defense
and Education Fund
99 Hudson Street
New York, NY 10013

Association of African American
People's Legal Council
13902 Robson Street
Detroit, MI 48227

Catholic Interracial Council of New York
899 Tenth Avenue
New York, NY 10019

Center for Democratic Renewal
P.O. Box 50469
Atlanta, GA 30302

Chinese for Affirmative Action
17 Walter U. Lum Place
San Francisco, CA 94108

Citizens' Commission on Civil Rights
2000 M Street, N.W., Suite 400
Washington, DC 20036

Commission for Racial Justice
105 Madison Avenue
New York, NY 10016

National Alliance Against
Racist and Political Repression
126 W. 119th Street, Suite 101
New York, NY 10026

National Association for the
Advancement of Colored People
74805 Mt. Hope Drive
Baltimore, MD 21215

National Institute Against
Prejudice and Violence
31 S. Greene Street
Baltimore, MD 21201

Southern Poverty Law Center
400 Washington Avenue
Montgomery, AL 36104

INDEX

Page numbers in *italics* refer to illustrations.